I0606403

My name is

This book is a gift from

May God the Father bless you.
May God the Son befriend you.
May God's Holy Spirit bring you

love
joy
peace
patience
kindness
goodness
faithfulness
gentleness and
self-control.

From the Bible

I was born on

I was baptized on

My godparents are

Written and compiled by Sophie Piper
Illustrations copyright © 2011 Caroline Williams
This edition copyright © 2011 Lion Hudson IP Limited

Published by
Lion Hudson Limited
Wilkinson House, Jordan Hill Business Park, Banbury Road, Oxford OX2 8DR, England
www.lionhudson.com

ISBN 978 0 7459 6251 1

First edition 2011

Acknowledgments
Every effort has been made to trace and contact copyright owners for material used in this book. We apologize for any inadvertent omissions or errors.

All unattributed prayers are by Sophie Piper and Lois Rock, copyright © Lion Hudson IP Limited.
The prayers by Victoria Tebbs and Mark Robinson are copyright © Lion Hudson IP Limited.

"Thank you, God, for sunshine" (p.17) by Mary Batchelor is © the estate of Mary Batchelor, used by permission.
The Lord's Prayer (p.50) as it appears in *Common Worship: Services and Prayers for the Church of England* (Church House Publishing, 2000) is copyright © The English Language Liturgical Consultation and is reproduced by permission of the publisher.

Bible extracts are taken or adapted from the Good News Bible published by the Bible Societies and HarperCollins Publishers, © American Bible Society 1994, used with permission.

Author Information/Bible References
p.2: Galatians 5
p.11: Traditional, from a New England sampler
p.13: Anonymous
p.14: Victoria Tebbs
p.17: Mary Batchelor
p.19: Mrs Cecil Frances Alexander (1818–95)
p.24: John Leland (1754–1841)
p.27: Traditional
p.29: Ralph Spaulding Cushman (1879–1960)
p.31: Katharine Tynan (1861–1931)
p.35: Julia Carney (1823–1908)
p.45: Philippians 2
p.47: Psalm 131
p.49: Psalm 23
p.59: Mark Robinson
p.64: Luke 18

A catalogue record for this book is available from the British Library

Printed and bound in China, April 2019, LH54

A Gift
For a Little Child's
BAPTISM

Sophie Piper

Illustrated by
Caroline Williams

LION
CHILDREN'S

Here I am

Before I was made,
God loved me.

When I was born,
God loved me.

Now I am here,
God loves me.

For ever and ever
God loves me.

Bless my hair and bless my toes
Bless my ears and bless my nose
Bless my eyes and bless each hand
Bless the feet on which I stand
Bless my elbows, bless each knee:
God bless every part of me.

c
a
b

Love

God bless all those that I love;
God bless all those that love me;
God bless all those that love
those that I love,
And all those that love those
that love me.

Love is giving, not taking,
mending, not breaking,
trusting, believing,
never deceiving,
patiently bearing
and faithfully sharing
each joy, every sorrow,
today and tomorrow.

The sun may shine
The rain may fall
God will always
Love us all.

Joy

Thank you, God, for sunshine,
Thank you, God, for spring,
Thank you, God, for sending
Every lovely thing.

All things bright and beautiful,
All creatures great and small,
All things wise and wonderful,
The Lord God made them all.

A summertime place
of trees and flowers,
the gentle call of a dove,
the hum of a bee –
these things must be
a glimpse of heaven above.

Peace

Hands together, close your eyes,
Pray to God above
That the night be filled with peace,
And the day with love.

Lord, keep us safe this night,
Secure from all our fears;
May angels guard us while we sleep,
Till morning light appears.

Now I lay me down to sleep,
I pray thee, Lord, thy child to keep;
Thy love to guard me through the night
And wake me in the morning light.

Patience

I will not hurry through this day;
I will take time to think and pray;
I will look up into the sky,
Where fleecy clouds and swallows fly:
And somewhere in the day, maybe
I will catch whispers, Lord, from thee!

O Year, grow slowly. Exquisite, holy,
The days go on.
With almonds showing, the pink stars blowing,
And birds in the dawn.

Grow slowly, year, like a child that is dear,
Or a lamb that is mild,
By little steps, and by little skips,
Like a lamb or a child.

When I'm tired of waiting
I will not whine or wail
I'll curl up very tightly
like a shyly sleeping snail.

When the time of waiting
goes on a long, long hour
I'll lift my head as slowly
as a shyly waking flower.

When the hours of waiting
seem they will never end
I'll put my hand in yours
because you're my forever friend.

Kindness

Little deeds of kindness,
Little words of love,
Help to make earth happy,
Like the heaven above.

Open my eyes
so I can see
the ways I could
more useful be.

Give me the strength
and heart and mind
to do the things
that are good and kind.

May angels guide me
through this day;
the paths unknown,
but blessed the way.

Goodness

Who made the sun?
Who made the day?
Who made the hours
for work and play?

God made them all,
God made them good,
God helps us live
the way we should.

A little seed
unfolds its leaves
and grows up to the light;
and I will lift
my face to heaven
and learn to do what's right.

May my life shine
like a star in the night,
filling my world
with goodness and light.

From the Bible

Faithfulness

I know I am only little.
I can't be in charge of big things.
But I know I am safe with you,
dear God:
as safe as a baby in its
mother's arms.

From the Bible

The Lord is my shepherd.
I'm safe in his care
by pools deep and still,
in green pastures so fair.

Whatever the danger,
whatever my fear,
God's love will surround me,
I'll know God is near.

His goodness and mercy
I trust will not end:
the Lord is my shepherd,
my helper and friend.

From the Bible

Our Father in heaven,
hallowed be your name,
your kingdom come,
your will be done,
on earth as in heaven.
Give us today our daily bread.
Forgive us our sins
as we forgive those who sin against us.
Lead us not into temptation
but deliver us from evil.

For the kingdom, the power,
and the glory are yours
now and for ever.

Amen.

Gentleness

Baby creatures, just awakened,
You are part of God's creation;
Baby creatures, oh so small,
God is father of us all.

I think the butterfly
says her prayer
by simply fluttering
in the air.

I think the prayer
of the butterfly
just dances up
to God on high.

May my hands be helping hands
For all that must be done
That fetch and carry, lift and hold
And make the hard jobs fun.

May my hands be clever hands
In all I make and do
With sand and dough and clay and things
With paper, paint and glue.

May my hands be gentle hands
And may I never dare
To poke or prod or hurt or harm
But touch with love and care.

Self-control

When I am in a temper
When I get really mad
I can be very dangerous
I can be very bad.

I'm wild as a tiger
I'm wild as a bear
I'm wilder than a wildebeest
And I don't even care.

Dear God who made the tiger
Dear God who made the bear
Please let me know you love me still
And that you'll always care.

May God bless all things wriggly
As wriggly as can be
Like worms and snakes and tadpoles
And, most of all, bless me.

Happy, noisy, quiet, sad
Often good and sometimes bad:
Through my ever-changing moods
Help me, God, to grow up good.

Jesus said,
"Let the children come to me
and do not stop them.
The kingdom of God belongs to
such as these."

From the Bible